THE ISLAND

THE ISLAND

Rosemary Canavan

STORY LINE PRESS

1994

Published by Story Line Press, Inc., Three Oaks Farm, Brownsville, OR 97327

This publication was made possible thanks in part to the generous support of the Nicholas Roerich Museum, the Andrew W. Mellon Foundation, the National Endowment for the Arts, and our individual contributors.

Book design by Chiquita Babb

Library of Congress Cataloging-in-Publication Data
—pending—

Acknowledgments

Acknowledgements are due to the editors of the following publications: *Poetry Ireland Review* No. 24 and 31, *Triskel Poets* 2 and 4, *Living Landscape Anthology,* the *Cork Yule Book, Traction News.*

To Michael

Contents

Part III

Part IV: The North

Part V: *Ringabella*

Part VI

Part *VII*

Singer

The mountains bred him.
Once, in the lark's eye
he strode moorland, lifted
silver fish in the still of the night.
Beached now on this grey city,
a rime of dust settles upon his brow;
dishevelled, tinkerish, he stares
beyond the pavement and the jostling crowd.
In that blue stare
the mountain memory remains:
those level eyes
recollect precision with the country task,
things done in the fitness of time,
work at the proper season,
movement in rhythm with trusted friends –
now remembered only in the old song.

PART I

English Market

Delightful
after the arid shelves
of the superstore,
the fish-stall man,
sleeves rolled,
plunges his arms into the slosh and scales
—that lost seaweed smell rises—
tumbling silver forms
to retrieve the prize.

A cheery fishwife
conversationally inclined
gives me a whole
salmon head for the cat.
Salmon of knowledge
—maybe I'll eat it myself—
gifts should never be
cast away.

Serpula Lachrymans

(Dry Rot)

Like a soft, furred creature
snuffling along floorboards
it secretly flourishes:
will its spores
penetrate my fingertips
if I reach out long enough,
to insulate me
from sorrows, frustration?

Its pale wool
shot with sulphur, with
rust-red, and fungi
peering like faces
from corners, look to
that dissolution we all
come to, lying by
Morpheus till each particle
flies from us
to rejoin the greater part,

will this
shroud us from sorrow
like your padded web?

Listen.
It pads along ceiling joists,
nuzzling firm grain
to char, crumble
until where wood was,

powder remains;
leaching towers to
shells staring skyward
through empty windows,
stones bare that were
dressed in silks and
ornamented for great men,
all bow
to this little creeping thing,
a knob on a thread,
remorselessly
weaving and twisting
with such energy
it must cry
"there is no death,
death's dead:"

for if decay
lives so, if
when one creature fails,
another grows, if all things
feed others, how
could we resent
shape-shifting
when our words
feed other heads,
our children
grow their children

so
let us dance
towards death,
sparks shivering
from our fingertips, blazing
mad glory like comets.

Nude

I should like to paint you
so you should never again say
your body shamed you, paint you
Bacchus, perhaps, lit in Italian sun,
a grape dipped in your suckling mouth;
or Dionysius, trailing ecstasy, for
Dionysius did not ape the muscle man,
and who would wish
to bed the grimmer Hercules?
Or paused in a clearing,
I would paint you
brown-skinned, slant-eyed,
the god Pan.

Portrait of Mr. S.H. at the
Project Theatre, Dublin

for Eugene

Laurelled with a bleached rook's nest
he soared ceilingward, crescent eyes
rising over horn-rimmed spectacles:
on his cragged face flesh
was like hummocks of turf undercut, he was
Green Man, vegetation god, you might
expect oak leaves antlering his skull,
words growing like vines from
his fingertips, his mouth, his chest:
we were foothills to his Carrantwohill
as "hello god" Theo said;
the mountain quaked softly with rumbustious laughter.

School-Crossing Lady, June

Amazon at the zebra crossing
she stands sunlit in early morning,
the prow of her bosom
jutting over the kerbstone,
her metal sign a standard
grasped to part a sea of cars,
and allow her charges
passage over the causeway.
Her hair like a plume
is quiffed in a disordered perm,
this patch of ground
quails under her authority.

Sea Widow

After the Piper Alpha disaster

In the night he comes to me
—shut out the dark night—
my dead love, burning and bloody,

become dark, terrible, a lover
riding the wings of morning,
his hair streaming in the cool wind,

the oil
flaring in great gouts below him,
a corolla of pain
casting lurid colour
on the dark water,

and the roar
as the rig went up
"O we knew, we knew," he cried
"as we shielded our faces
from the white wall of flame,
and the sudden agony, gone again
as the dark quiet suddenly came,"

so leave me, neighbours, friends,
women bearing tea and quiet talk
to soothe pain; it is
in the night, in the night
he comes to me.

Wreckage

I

Day
revealed your eyes,
deep, shy like a child's,
a retiring philosopher.

Lie with me,
this time I will—
you hesitate:
don't say "yes, yes",
lie gently;
I will stroke your brow
and call to you
saying "come to me now, now".

II

Solicitous for my working
you advise me;
never fear,
I have found my touchstone:
this man
is where my two worlds meet.

III

Kerry
is where two worlds meet
uncertainly,
trembling along
the smooth-stoned beach,
the shimmering water's edge;

And will you ever
kiss salt-caked lips, taste
the sweet salt between my thighs?
No, aeons of loneliness
separate the me, you from us.

IV

Your absence
sunders me, seeding distrust,
making me question now
what seemed to be truthfulness
yet
craving familiarity with your touch
I ache to tongue the warm cave of your mouth,
hear your blood drumming an advance,
mine beating in recompense,
this time there'll be no drawing back.

V

Shipwrecked
I scan the sky
yet when you, rescuing, come,
like a cruel twist in a dream
the truth leaks out, and
the end's sour,
commonplace,
not worth waiting for.

Lovers near Bogland

What would you do, my dear,
if we lived when lovers were taken out
and slaughtered, following the discovery?

As naked we stood shivering in the night air
ringed by hostile eyes, terror-struck
when we realised their cold determination,
would you deny our secret union still?
Or would you, towards the end
when all reprieve was lost, turn
and tell me your love in a low voice
before the knife cut:
hold my eyes, smiling across the gap
as they took us, separately, to the execution?

I think I would.

PART II

The Island

The Island

28th May, 1848. ...we came to anchor ... within five hundred
yards of Spike Island—a rueful looking place, where I could dis-
cern, crowning the hill, the long walls of the prison, and a battery
commanding the harbour.

May 29th: In this court, nothing is to be seen but the high walls
and the blue sky. And beyond these walls I know is the beautiful bay
lying in the bosom of its soft green hills. If they keep me here for
many years I will forget what the fair outer world is like. Gazing on
grey stones, my eyes will grow stony.

John Mitchell, Jail Journal

I The Journey

First
there is a web of bridges and islands
round like breasts, like
a child's drawing of hills:
from here the island is beautiful,
you cannot see
that the shape on the summit
is a stone bastion.

When the boat bore me
first to the pier, the sea
was glowing unearthly blue,
the island glittered,
it was crystal, wind-scoured
in the blinding morning sun,
a place to see mysteries,
Inis Pic of the monks.

It seemed less blessed later,
under a grey, troubled sky, as swans

clustered by the lee of the island
and the dark swell broke high;
or past Haulbowline, mist-hung
with the far shore gone,
and buoy struts at low water
outposts of a bleak, forgotten land:
or by the ruined fortifications
of the old magazine, where
a ghostly redcoat might leap
to challenge, not knowing
the passage of time.

Sometimes the place
fills with ghosts, crowding
upon me, as the living leave,
until the soft thrudd of the launch's engines
wakes me to walk to the pier's edge.

II Embarked

Her wake is a sure arabesque
as she pulls past Cobh and across
to the long finger of quay.
Stilts rise, gaunt, barnacled,
greenish at low tide
as she bangs the bottom step
and we jump, smartly,
before she swings out again.

Beyond the beach of brick and sea-worn shards,
the blind cottages of the old village:
street corners deserted, clean,
bear testimony to conversation
long since snatched by the wind;
and in neglected gardens
bushes by the old walls
this spring are filled with birdsong:
singing to the incarcerated
they torture, and still exhilarate.

But our steps pull free, up,
as the bay revealed under us
is blue as a kingfisher's wing.
And soaring our spirits skim
the margin of wooded hills,
miniature as a magic lantern scene.
Until suddenly between two grass banks
the gates loom: we are let in.

III The Enclosure

Inside these walls, you cannot see the world.
Save at the edges, the great enclosure
is bare of buildings, a moon-bleak
surface of cinders and mud
that dries to yellow dust
in the spring air; yet
despite shadows of unease,

the shuttered form of the old jail,
or the burned-out block,
today is workmanlike, spellings
are learned, business is sorted out,
a kind of reality is touched
as the sun falls upon
the geranium in the English room.

IV To Travel Beyond The Confines

But in Dublin the wind cuts sharp,
on this ground exploring is dangerous:
search even innocently, and you might
scrape flesh, touch bone.
Behind the grime-streaked stone
that towers above the house backs,
lime-cauled bodies of heroes burn,
and sounding above
the engines at rush hour
the cries of the lost women—
slashing, slashing—
and blood trickling
under the cell door.

She is not like the others:
withdrawn, she contemplates
an open book as morning breaks,
lighting the chipped plaster
patterning her living space.

Yet, with only time
and the monthly sign
to mark the passing of her womanhood,
how much more
could she, undestroyed, contain?
—not much more—
so given that one chance, she let them
mount her behind the sacristy; was it
joy worth waiting for, to feel
that brief shudder of pleasure
before the grey walls closed her in again?
Her body was fresh and sweet still, cream
against the dark triangle,
but her face had a greyed look,
and scored deep under her eyes
shadows sank by the cheek bone.

V The Lazarhouse

So what's to be done
to stop him fucking
when he's let out
of the unit for prisoners
with Aids antibodies?
Condoms are disallowed
by the authorities
and the girls
not knowing
don't say no.

VI The Female Ward

And in the female section
even the copybooks are bleeding,
blotted and blotched on the yellow covers
with tears, with browned blood
(those pools, are they edged with orange, are they magenta?)
For the women, not content
to bleed with the moon
slash and hack
at the whitish flesh
till stones redden under the flood
—where's her copybook?
—Miss, her copybook
is all covered in blood...

VII The Class

In the hushed room
we form a circle, to read
that remembering pigeons, he tells
how the bird, released from the boy's hand
soars—real far—
out of the cage on the smoky roof.
It is afternoon. Locked
in the foetid air we fight
sleep and dream of release;
and when the evening train

pulls at last between rounded hills
I would press my head against them, for peace.

VIII *Leaving*

Evening, on the island.
As I reach the quay,
walking on wet seaweed
that the last storm has thrown
carelessly, along the stone
(brown pods, popped
by my boots) I stare
under the rain-pocked surface
of the sea, where clouds
mirrored in grey billow
like ectoplasm, and a goat's
head, then a bull
grotesque as the Minotaur
peer briefly, horridly: then
disappear, and I search
desperately over grey water
for the launch to rescue me.

IX *To View From a Distance*

Seaward of Cork
islands at evening time are glass-green
stones inlaid upon sapphire, upon aquamarine,

and great ships move in arcs around headlands
gliding and silent on the estuary:
and the island is enclosed, secret,
gleaming softly in slanting light.

Island of the blessed? These poor
inherit space in a stone dormitory, seek
oblivion in a needle or drink,
with only the grave to end
the tortured wandering of a damaged mind.

On the island there is a graveyard
where the graves are numbered,
featureless. They never left:
but as I leave
from far away it becomes
only an island,
shimmering in the white of early morning,
lovely at evening time.

Joe in Jail

Oh, Joe
with the brown skin,
teak-coloured curls, and lips
cherubic, serene
like a Medici page boy;

you shrug, cheerfully,
when someone taunts
you sleep with men

(at ease in here)

outside, will you
pillow your face
(deep breath)
in the white bag again

and the fumes make
strange images come in your brain
and your limbs
dance dance like a madman's—

what use to you then
is the geography—Primary III—
you took with such delight
and pored over
for a whole afternoon?

Orderly

Meeting him unexpectedly
as rain lashed the parade ground,
he seemed shrunken
into the rough-weave coat: his face
was glazed grey, his knuckles blue
that had pulled fish-filled
nets, steered the boat
to windward and back:
as "new job" he said wryly,
nodding at cart and rubbish bins
he trailed, coolie-style, to the block.
The last one doing that job was simple.
And yet, from the deadened skin
his eyes light to me:
lights of grey at the temple,
eyes blue like seas.

The Custodians

Look at their eyes. You can see it
most of all in the older ones, those
whose blooding came years ago;
men thick-set like bulldogs, they
know the worst in you just by looking.
Eyes, they say, are openings to the soul:
their eyes are dead, cold, void, as if
the lost heart had splintered over
to ice at the core: they
will supervise blooding the young ones
when an inmate goes too far.

Sometimes Low Light

Sometimes low light catches faces
and lifts them suddenly to beauty:
as in the earnestness of faces
at a community meeting in '72
by the Peaceline in Belfast;
or once, at a university
concert, when a girl
bright-haired as a Botticelli angel
was lit in a doorway against dark wood;
or once, in a young convict listening
to a prison concert: his gold curls
framed the bitter vacancy of his face.

Spring Cleaning

The governor has decreed
a full-scale poisoning of cats.
An island's tidier without animals.

Death
to the silhouette that slinks and struts
from the shadow of a parade ground bush,
to the shaggy marmalade
that fixes you, suddenly owl-like,
from a tuft of grass,
to the mottled tortoiseshell
that slips, brief as a ghost,
down the backyard path,
to those that cross and recross
the invisible cat-paths by my window;

death
        death
                death
                        death:

a tidy island, without animals.

Slipway

It is easy to slip
to a life where work
becomes as inevitable as sleep,

each morning leaving
at the same hour with all the others
past a sunlit, empty studio,

indeed, lately learning punctuality
I don't even miss the boat:

and though time off for funerals
is probably the biggest cause
of lost working hours in Ireland
I don't know anybody dead

so weave the morning helter-skelter
with other uptight drivers; we career
past shivering water, shield our eyes
from sunrise over the reeds, the ghostly fire
of blackthorn flowers in hedgerows.

He told me, "when my heart goes cold, I want blood".
And I dreamed myself mother-slayer, drained
bitch whose dugs would nurture
no new cities: like a great wheel
these days blur, and I cannot tell
how much is true, how much
dream image that I waking would reject.

Winter Light

On the Owenabue estuary
dawn and dusk leap red,
and even factory chimney smoke
is a wraith, coral and white,
wreathed with morning mist.
And Spike looks like Stalag Luft III, as
two men in rough brown overcoats
with collars turned up round their cropped heads,
cross the bare ground beyond the prison gate.

PART III

The Chapel

He was slender, and
I should not have remembered
your broad body
when my arms circled him:
nor how we lay
side by side, not touching,
beyond the high window of the balcony:
northwards, there was a
wall of rock, and
to the south, the sea.
Where we lay
was a chapel, naved
like hands praying, it was
clutched in a rock cleft;
you had forged it
from a stone shed,
given it sanctity
by contemplation, fruit
of your loneliness,
which it was
not for me to relieve.

We, turned aside to sleep

Sometimes you walk where I cannot follow you

We had walked into the garden
the big man and I
when suddenly
he was in my bed
wearing only navy-blue underpants
His great bear-body
was hot and comforting
until you knocked at the door
and I tried to shake him off
but he was so heavy, so heavy—
and he did not seem to hear
when I pleaded with him

I had nothing to wear

so pulled on a short jacket
it did not cover one of my breasts
and I had to leave the caravan
where we stayed
and cross a field
which was sky-blue studded with pools of concrete
where boys were playing hurley
(whether they saw my one exposed breast
I do not know)
to reach the house where you and the children
were making breakfast

On the veranda a hag with snow-white hair accosted me
could she use my oven to bake cakes for the hurley team?
I was angry at her intrusion
but she knew what I had been doing
so it was difficult to refuse

I do not know if I ever gained the kitchen

But I was walking in the fast lane
of a four-lane highway
the road was broad, deserted
except for a woman in a small car
who wanted to pull out left from a turning
she waited until I had walked by

and then I was turning, turning, scraping inside
a great womb-shaped piece of white clay
beating a fork around to make it perfectly smooth
the outside was ribbed
I touched it with a finger
and it was searing, white-hot from the fork's friction
at my touch it collapsed to a little low teapot
covered with fine coils of white clay like curls
it was no bigger than the palm of my hand

Sometimes where I walk you cannot follow me

Pieta

Not beer, not blow, but your body
intoxicates me, O man of the wild
locks; there is no lack of
Magdalenes to wipe fingers
down your sweat, but I would
drink it from that little cup
under your neck, that shows
over your sweater's ragged black rib:

and though your song seems
coarsened now, and I believed
I'd built up hedges barbed
with tongues of thorn
against you, still you break
through, proffering friendship, to wake
beauty with a kiss; as "Your face!"
he said, wondering, "Your face!"
—and that morning my lips burned,
eyes glowed, there was
no need to colour it—

and when moth-struck, I blunder back
each time you break my banks, though
I bury you with fresh earth,
blot you from conscious reckoning,
yet you occur in flash-backs;
though I search to find
what would heal wings,
what soil might sprout indifference,

or what banishing ritual
could strike
your image from my heart.

Travelling Poet

If you
forgetting again my birthday
should take the road
with my books
and your few possessions
stowed in your ruck-sack,
remember this: contempt is not
only bred by familiarity;
and a butt-end
is not the best thing to remember you by.

Ars Longa

Notes from a Lost Recipe Book

Imprinted at the headquarters
of the Women's Institute (the Northern Ireland
War Memorial Building, in Waring Street, Belfast)
this dough-stained, finger-printed booklet
holds all those women who worshipped
at the low dark church on the hill:

women with bare honest faces, imbued
with that peculiar Northern gentleness,
their forearms stout enough to cream butter and sugar,
their speech sings the rough music of the place,
women of Gilnahirk, Cullybackey, Loughbrickland,
Newtownbreeda, Maheragall, Carnmoney, all those
Hannas, Boyds, Craigs, McCoubreys
leave this as evidence of their art:

And did Miss S. Donaldson's
Sultana Biscuits catch her a farmer,
as Miss Margaret Parkhill's Mince Roll vied
with Mrs. Wilson's Salmon Surprise? Did
Mr. McGarry recoil at Beetroot Mould, even
when garnished with ham, cold meat
and salad? Did Mr. Stewart take
advantage of Olive's Melting Moments,
when she served them for late night supper
with tea and bread? What if
Walnut Fancies or Coffee Kisses greeted
the commercial traveller? Might
Ruby Gillespie promise Paradise Cake?

O the riches of Apple Foam Dessert, Pear Upside-down
Pudding, fadge, fushies, colcannon and ginger slab:
they might titter at Kiss-me-quick Pudding and French chews
over a bowl of Mutton broth, but instead
content themselves with fare as simple
as Miss G. Dunwoody's Rough Wheaten Bread.

Visitation

Could they see the print
of our faces on the window
when they returned, those
dwellers in our old house?
"Some sort of hippies," my father
said, seeing the crocheted rug
on the sofa, its many colours
spangling the dull light of the kitchen.
Did they love to live
enfolded by those stone walls
knitted with cow's hair, hare's blood?
Were they uneasy as dark came
(That the woman at the stair's head)?
Did their children hear boards
shrink and creak towards nightfall,
hide heads under blankets
and still not shut out the fear?

Offering

Do not hold it against me
if I should praise your mother,
and that stumbling we walked
a treacherous path to discover
the bitter-sweet nature of mother—
daughter love; such predicaments
are not peculiar to us;
and in lieu of myself I bring
three children to you: death
and circumstance have deprived
them of any other grandmother.
They come to you with trust:
hold them, gather them to you;
when you are old, when you are gone
they will praise you,
speak your epitaph, in
the continuum of our experience.

The Paranoid

She did not scream aloud
but there was a scream
echoing around her head
that fell, then rose like a
depth charge

as children
tore her flesh and ate it
and friends grinned, mocking her
—she could see
their friendship was a mask

but she grinned back
like a cur
wagging its tail for scraps:
you scream like this
when you are caught, and
there is no way out.

Photograph Album

And so you sat, dear white-haired lady
stranded from a time
when girls were 'gels'
and little nursery words—
'Steady the Buffs' to the wavering toddler—
betrayed the colonial heritage.

Your Chivelston drawingroom:
Christopher Robin in the piano stool,
and 'Little Black Sambo' my first storybook,
whose tigers turned to 'ghee'—mysterious word
to one who never learnt the sahib talk.

Here, garlanded with great-grandchildren, you sat
frail yet contented by a sunlit wall.
That near the end; turning back
I unlock others' remembrances
in the brown-leaved book:

That maiden in boater and Edwardian lace,
and earlier, wave-haired child posed in fancy-dress;
a delicate mother in teagown bent over her first,
then fading as children took precedence
in the photographs.

Such gentleness
I remember more than anything;
could I have sat, gentle, at your deathbed
dear grandmother, I might not now

as I still do
feel your loss, fear
that this photograph album is all I have left of you.

Newt

I remember
sun slanting into umber depths
and the swift flicker
as a small creature, disturbed,
sent tremors of sediment
over the pond base

and when I saw the newt,
his eyes jewelled, iridescent,
poised like a miniature dragon
on our stone kitchen floor,

infant, I seemed to remember
so long ago a plant-fringed pool
—or perhaps that was some other garden,
similarly sunlit, composed, serene,
impossibly permanent.

Early City, Douglas Road

Arrowing towards morning
two swans overhead:
white necks outstretched,
wings white on the down
beat; behind them sky
drops to meet grey city streets.

Evening

Two lights: a cottage
Set upon rising ground,
Clumped around it
Are black masses of trees.
They curve their long dark crooked fingers
To shelter the house
(Like a flame from the wind)
Behind the trees the sky is pale and
Dark sweeps of grey.

PART IV

The North

Incident near the New Lodge

Once I heard
bullets winging past me
with a low whine
like you'd hear in a cowboy film:
it was in a street
between the New Lodge Road
and Tiger's Bay, the bullets
were probably not aimed at me.

A Brief Encounter with Murder

She talked.
She should not have done that.
And so the iron hand lifts gun to head.

Like a rabbit she cowers, shuddering.
Her fear disgusts him, he is ready
to make steel burrow into soft flesh.
Deciding, he tightens the index finger.

The explosion releases him to normality.
Turning his back on the spilled blood, flesh
he leaves swiftly. Later he will
clean and replace the gun, treat himself
to a cigarette, a cup of coffee.

No Message

For a woman who said no-one has ever written about the North

We bloody told youse
(old soldiers, we told youse)
time and again
with our twisted bodies, our
blood spattering on pavements,

marched, sang it
to tourists, television reporters,
spoke stories, poems, the voices of infants,
stood on stage and performed it;

(were you ever afraid? — Yes,
during a riot, of falling,
or walking at evening, of
bullets thudding between my shoulder blades)

O we cried it
in ditches and churchyards
told you
with a thousand voices
but you wouldn't listen

so don't
shout Yell O to me
I've listened
too long, lady.

Drum Beat: The Eleventh Night

The Falls, 1973

Red brick spreads out from under the mountain,
fanned like a deck of cards below the slope,
chequers of slate are glimmering wet on the rooftops
down to the silent waters of the Lough.

And the leaden air trembles like drumskin,
a pall of menace hangs with the bonfire smoke.
See—our nerves are wound back to the breaking,
ears strained for the ghost of a wrong note.

Last night we were sitting over the tea-things,
windows open overlooking the park;
then came the sudden clack clack of gunfire—
someone had been shot down in the dark.

Now I think that I hear the Lambegs' rumble,
faint cries from the dancers in the street:
stout flows as fever pitch comes closer,
whiskey quickens the tongue and taps the feet.

Over on this side, the charge finds no conductor,
stillness brimming the streets as the drumming starts:
drinking here is hurried, to reach oblivion:
if the long knives come, they will find an empty heart.

Mise Eire

St. Patrick's Eve, 1988

A sanitised nationalism
is all that's permitted us,
enough to play O'Riada on Patrick's night:

the old melodies, seditious, defiant,
sounding strangely
through the orchestral accompaniment;

(tunes you could hear
rasped out in a smoky pub
or a shebeen down the Falls)

as shots zoom in
on heroes of 1916, their faces
touched up to lifelikeness,

so the dead
seem to leap out at us
from the faded, familiar images.

A horn calls, distant, muted: a bugle,
then a trumpet bells
the shrill clarity of belief,

and pictures of ancient gunrunning at Howth
(a woman, well-dressed, seated,
holding a Mauser) recall

they are still searching
bushes, outhouses, bogland
for the cargo of the Exeunt.

The fat American, immaculate
despite a light beading of sweat,
conducts obedient instruments,

as a but gouts fire, and cars
flaming on Catherine wheels
appear to fuel the inevitable climax:

and the young—always the young—
it seems the same young dark-haired men
have been running down the Falls

for the last twenty years,
fleeing guns, or firing petrol-bombs
down a road littered with half-bricks

O it's terrible, terrible, terrible, as

respectable as Americans, we anticipate
gaudy floats, the young goose-pimpled majorettes
tramping the same songs out.

And who best but the
headmaster over unruly Northerners
to lecture the futility of violence—

Does he know something we don't?

While the Black Gang gun three in Gib
and three go down at the funeral
and another two die, caught by the crowd;

and the sons of Ulster and the Army
mark it out with liberation armies
through a hundred shades of red,

and gable ends like Cassadra
cry O terrible terrible—
it is not yet come to the worst.

PART V

Ringabella

Crab Apples

There used to be skylarks, he said:
we would lie
on the flat of our backs
in summer, to listen,
and in the hedgerows,
crab apples.

But the fifty acre field
grows no hedgerows where
birds might flutter and perch:
no corncrake rasps to break
the still air above
the sileaged grass,
and the skylark's song
no longer tumbles
to the fields and woods
round Ringabella.

Sowing Spring Barley

I

Today that long flank of hill
which flamed gold, as the
stubble burned, only a week ago,
gapes in the wake of the six-blade plough.

The wet flesh of mother land is
brown as an African's, soft, rich and deep,
then dries to russet in the evening wind;
gulls sing demented for greed, as furrows
stand line upon line in the reddening sun

while the great machines hum and whine
(two ploughing at once
drive at each other, pass and return
time and time again in the hillside):

dusk falls, and still the engines grind
and headlights pass and pass each other again
when the hill's too dark to be seen
under the dim sky of the evening.

II

A generation ago, to lure
growth from the soil was a week's work
for four men, a horse, a plough;

now, in one evening, a man
impenitent on the huge machine
carves this great wound upon the land.

Towards Minane

How should we guess
who is the holiest?

So count yourself blessed
in this land where a crosier's
not a shepherd's hook
but something you get a belt of,

if the old roadman, grinning
a mouthful of crooked raw teeth
as he looks up from the brambles
and long grass, should lift
his stained fingers, bishop-like, in salute,
raise his billhook in benison.

Notes for a Landscape:
November Evening

They are watercolour clouds, sponged
rose and palest indigo
in the broad sky beyond my window.
Under them, trees on the low summit
are inked in fine sharp strokes
that blur and run
as the dark moves upward
from the fields and hedges of my neighbour's farm.
Cloud in loose chequers
moves across the sky, and
impelled by the freshening east wind,
a rose bush twig, bare
of all except one wizened leaf, beats
a staccato morse upon my window pane.

The Rationalist

Only an old pishogue, he said
when I told him I would use a water diviner
to search out the best spring:
yet revealed himself by voice and features
a true West of Ireland countryman;
scratch him and you wouldn't have to go
far down to find pishoguery in plenty,
or discover under the cloak of the new God
old ones, playing catch-me-if-you-can.

Dusk

It is only at
dusk honey-
suckle breathes
sweet breath: at
dusk cattle rear
and charge in
darkening fields:
at dusk trees
blur, become
unreal, as song
from thrushes,
blackbirds arrows
through air:
at dusk wind
drops, dew falls,
moths stir.

Cottage Interior:
Towards Winter

Cold looms from shadows, but
under this wide arch
the fire holds me: gold flame
lights the room like an incantation,
and though the wind howls
at the broken door beyond the porch,
this night I am sound against weather;
and my dog, curled
on the warm stone where the ash falls,
snores, contented.

Country Funeral

I

Evening, in early autumn.
The countryside
was washed light gold
by the lowering sun, and
all the lines and furrows in the land stood out.
The stillness of it all!
as we paused to wait
for the coffin from Cork: only
a woman in red cardigan, low-
voiced, leaned at the window
of a neighbour's car.

II

"Your neighbour's drowned!" she
cried, running on. We were
by the gate, talking. "Drowned?"
"At the Ferry Point, not an hour ago…"
True, cars were gathering
by the cottage where he lived,
the guard's arrival emphasised disaster,
and later, as I watched helplessly,
the ambulance passed
above the hedges
bearing the drowned body to the city.

III

At first meeting,
I thought him testy. My child
had plucked the white valerian
he had been watching for the seed,
leaving only crimson flowers
lining the low wall
along the roadside by the Ferry Point.

IV

Cars trailed the switchbacked road
at walking pace: on higher ground
rooks cawed in the oak trees;
inside the churchyard
the smell of crushed grass
and evergreens, and a river
gabbled in sunlight.
After the rites, the prayers
that dropped into our silence
as we ringed the grave,
sullen with bewilderment,

young men stepped out,
and casting off their Sunday coats,
rolled sleeves and grasped
long spades to fill the grave:
the clods of earth

rang off the coffin wood
hollowly.

V

Hard to imagine, under
that earth, that wood,
the beetle-browed head,
dipped as he looked at you
with wry humour: the shoulders
ox-broad, his hand huge
from sawing, or pushing the plane
over untutored wood;
and to know that he would never see
the seeds of the white valerian
bloom on the wall
above that fatal water.

Summer: South Cork

Old men with
billhooks and bent-brimmed hats
lean to the rank growth
by the roadside;
roundels of hogweed
are rich as cream
and the scent of meadowsweet
is on the air;
foxgloves proclaim
the spell of summer evenings,
while mid-distance, waist-high in grass,
a lone reaper, like
Time, scythes the hay.

His Sexuality, Almost Forgotten

The old virgin farmer
remembers helping a neighbouring wife
through a back window
(her key forgotten),
and as she lifted her leg
to the window frame
her skirt blossomed in the wind like a flower
so that her plump thighs were revealed
and the curve of her pudenda,
perceptible though cloth-concealed;
this he recalls
by the fire's blaze
or in conversation with
bachelors, or a woman
wicked enough not to be offended.

Tide Turn

Soon it will be
evening on the Back Strand,
and I am perched
upon a rock to watch the tide come in:

There is a pause, and next
small waves begin to lick
the tips of rock reaching into the strand,
then rush with wild eddies of flung sand
upon rockpools which since the last tide
were mirror-still, jewelled
by seaweeds and small animals.

A miniature catastrophe! I think
of storms, hurricanes,
typhoons, earthquakes, volcanoes,
and of man, fragile as a may
fly, who in one day
must feed, reproduce and die,

and delighting in my airy fragility
I curl toes into rock cracks,
(my spirit silk-light as fly wings)
and exult that I, amid
such a pantheon of disaster
am alive this calm and sun-filled day
to watch a small wave
(as the tide turns)
licking weedy rocks.

PART VI

Poem

His skin shone, moon-
pale, that evening as
he held me pleadingly.
Lord of women
he could be
yet he will not
lord it over me;
let him hold back,
contain his urgency,
I am his
on loan only,
never in perpetuity.

From a Parked Car

When I saw you yesterday
stepping out into that bitter wild wind
your hair spread out round your head like a halo
as you pulled your coat closer around your body
and turned to salute me,
a move rehearsed to look casual
and so with the artificiality of a dancer.

And I stay back
separated by such a distance,
only my eyes move out to you
and my hand lifts up,
two divers in diving bells
saluting each other
across a bitter sea.

A Parting

I watched the plane curve
perilously upwards, engines
streaming twin trails of black smoke
with you, my daughter, inside it:
and it was as if the cord
was cut all over again,
I was amazed that pain
could be so violent, sharp,
severing: and turning
knew this to be
the first of many departures.

Night Watch

Sleeping,
in angel innocence she lies:
shut, the dark-lashed eyes,
so smooth her golden brow
you might think her now
tinted marble, deftly styled,
not a warm, soft-breathing child.
Look, the little nose
and mouth, a perfect bow
over the small firm chin—
my daughter, no changeling,
even if possessed
of a faery waywardness.
Awake, full of merriment:
in sleep, how innocent—
nothing to me more fair
as I gaze on her sleeping there.

Reply, to Casanova

"Man's love is of man's life a thing apart
'Tis woman's whole existence."

Byron, Don Juan cxciv

You talked
as if a quaint jester,
anarchist at the centre of your world
pressed upward against my thigh:

apologetic for its extravagant demonstration
of what was, after all, your own intention,
you, conveniently, are unable
to effect
any attempt at moderation.

While I understand
your difficulty
and that its lack of conscience
in no way reflects your own mature humanity,
I find myself
unable to yield to such necessity

after all
I am a woman, and
my sex (sweet sir)
is at the heart of me.

Harvest

And even
stones have spirits:
these three, garnered
from Ballyheigue—
the white, the pierced,
the circled one—
put away now on a shelf
wrapped softly in winter dust,
await a touch, a light breath
(like seeds sleeping in winter)
to reveal in a wild burst
their imprisoned life.

Crow Clouds

Crow clouds
over a mottled dawn
grass stirs
cattle lie down
and inland
seabirds
presaging a storm.

Chernobyl

What bitterness I felt
as the poison spread
country by country,
making the young green of Spring
a parody of perfection,
sun fell
on the new flowers
and we dared not touch them.

Nature too breeds catastrophe,
but there is no bitterness
in surrendering to the rush
of flood water, perhaps,
once the first terror is past;
swept in exhilaration
till sense sleeps
and the wave enfolds you,
body in the immensity
of the world deep.

The Union

"Heaven and Earth are ruthless"
Tao Te Ching

I was walking the quay that evening
by the Heuston Station reach, watching how
bridges over the Liffey made circles underneath,

and Dublin in dusty rose and grey
was like and old lady hurrying along the quayside—
brittleboned, faded, respectable—

when breaking the oily current
something like an elbow, long-drowned,
bobbed up, down, then

a long white belly scythed the water
as the creature reared a snout
that was mottled, whiskered, shining-skinned:

the seal glanced darkeyed on
the upper world, then dipped
to re-emerge with a mullet in its jaws;

there began a deadly pas de deux
with the fish held, let go, then again caught
in the cold clutch of rounded paws

over and under in the reedy water,
till it paused to raise
its black, human-seeming gaze

and I saw what sailors knew,
that the souls of the drowned
called to you from seal's eyes

that were vortices, drawing you
to deep water, to join
that fatal pas de deux with the seal.

Wood Woman

Perhaps I shall hide in the wood's heart
in a strong-walled, low stone house,
the trees hung about me with silence;
until I become a crazy old lady—
my black bosom heaving, a bush
of thorn-grey hair to crown me—
I should rage, shrilly, at strangers,
guard with fanatic jealousy
my hoard of worm-holed furniture,
cracked cups, old scraps of cloth,
and drifts of mouldering ancient newspapers.

Peacock Passage

for Catherine

At first the chalky minaret
pennanting my Ford bonnet
puzzled me: then I remembered
your lordly bird passing who
took this for pedestal;
was honoured by his gift, insignia
from arse of emerald and lapis lazuli.

Blackbirds

She
a little brown
sinuous creature,
alert as her
black-backed mate:
he chipper,
sleek as a priest,
snake-like in the
probing pick of his beak
at the warm earth:
they pluck worms
like currant from cake.

Who is he?

Nursery Verses for a Valentine Card

Is he the King of England crowned?
An Indian chief of great renown?
A Chinese in a Coolie hat,
A stubborn Russian Diplomat?
A Venetian Doge? A City Gent?
A Polar Explorer in a tent?
A portly Vicar taking tea,
A Doctor of Philosophy?
A Pirate with an evil leer,
A swanky self-made Millionaire,
A Bishop? Or don't tell me he's
A Member of the Secret Police?
Is he a Monk with tonsured crown,
A Tripper in a Seaside Town,
A Jockey in his Racing Gear,
A famous Roman Emperor?
A super sleuthing Private Eye,
A Jolly Tar who'll Do or Die,
A Saint?
     A Scholar?
          —no, it's only
P*rcy feeling rather lonely.

After

And you filled me
Deep with the very surge of life
A rich river flows in my veins
My head blooms like a flower
I am strong with a strange soft strength
And my body moves like a moon-walker
Dancing upon the earth.

Poem in Two Languages

Quand tu me touche
avec tes doigts d'un ouvrier;
dur, maix si doux
quand tu me touche

and I watch, amazed
those square palms
and splay-tipped fingers,
so deft with the trade tools,
economical of gesture
to complete
the master piece

and I am past watching
as those fingers trace over my skin
each tip drawing
a curl of flame
to the tinder place,
so soft I cannot tell
where your skin starts, mine ends:
so perfectly they blend,

quand tu me touche
avec tes doigts d'un ouvrier:
dur, maix si doux
quand tu me touche.

Pub Talk

Once again I have come to collect you,
and you sit there, despite promises,
with great water-logged eyes
like a sick dog

and a half-smile twitches your lips a little
(uncertain whether to be facetious, or apologetic)
and your face is flushed, and a little greasy
where the light bulb picks you out against peeling walls

and I wish I was anywhere but here,
calling you to come home,
sad shepherd in the golden evening.

Hurricane: East England

That night the wind
put lips to chimneys and
to window crevices, leant
close and cried, "Hoo!"
howled eerie and sorrowful
as it whirred and flew
around the house: such a
wild torrent of air
that only the sooty
innocent faces of
chimney sweeps knew
why this visitation was made
on a land which, sleeping,
seemed the model
of peace, of plenty.

The storm cackled over rooftops,
hissed disdain of
planning regulations as it
knocked church spires, snapped
Wealden coppices like matchsticks,
downed great trees that hummed
and sang all summer as sap
travelled from root to
branch and back again;
now swathes of branches
bound the roadsides,
and roots, death-stiffened,
clutch at empty air.

And folk who trimmed
and clipped the hedges round
their bungalows ("I like to keep it
nice and tidy") stand back
and scratch heads at the giants
that strew parkland like a battlefield:
they're deadwood now, their corpses
seasoning in the storms of winter
are crops for carpenters, not gardeners.
"Some time it'll take," they say,
"to tidy up the mess that's left,"
and there's a glut
of firewood, now, in the Home Counties.

Old Landscape: West Cork

In autumn
the enamelled hills
glint russet and gold
between grey ribs of rock.
Such complexity:
stone and valley
interlocked
as if plaited
by peasant fingers.
Humps of hill
rise to fill the sky
or dapple the background
indigo, turquoise,
to smoke-blue horizon.
Stitched into place
sheets of burning emerald
where farmer's labour
from rock and bracken hollows
wrought fertility.
Wild goats against the sky:
fox stealthy under bracken:
stoat a streak of red fur into the bramble:
small birds wheeling and counter-wheeling;
all move to the ancestral pattern
as they did when the hermit monks
admired them, sense honed
by their loneliness.

Approaching Swindon, Probably

They are not like us, I thought,
as I watched the English girls
with faces like painted dolls,
and expressions cultured
to the right degree of indifference.
Then, over the rocking aisle
of the express train, I saw
a mother clutching her child
with primeval tenderness, and knew
suddenly that under the skin they too
were savages: afraid of the dark,
touching for luck, believing in miracles.

PART VII

The Quarrel

the day was
white hot, the sky
glared

a bird   tossed notes
from one bush
another
answered it

was it my time
to be immobile
while children explored
noisily?

I wanted
never to move

the sun   lapped me
there was a soft sound
of wind and water

our pain was far away
seemed washed

bushes bore
candle-catkins, sun-lit

it took
two children to go
exploring, learn the lore

of dock-leaf cure
for nettles

I moved alone
when I was child

a cloud of flies
trembled on the wind
wavering
like a moment in time
play of light on their wings

the languorous smell of may

I found
a nut, a bird's
flecked egg shell ripped
where the fledgling had come out

free
I could look wind-tossed, weather-beaten

fish turned lazily

my King
you wounded yourself

crucially

are we
back on the cliff edge?

A Song for the Visitors

For Robert

In Moyvane's pub
the wind-burned faces
opened, and voices
clear as larks
came carrolling out.
One man in particular
caught your glance:
"In America
he would not escape notice."

His singing is free. For cash
he would not sing like that.

My Ireland

With her own hands, she wove it:
with their bodies, they wove it,
bearing mute testimony
to this matter of principle:
we have fallen far
from the Fates guiding destiny
to a woman weaving her own hangrope.

Night after night in the dim cell,
she wove strands she had
stolen from the knitting class.
The noose was her own work.
Others had caught her in a noose
she could not flee, fettering her
with the sentence of 'Poverty'.

And that other girl, was she
more tragic than the rest?
She had monied parents, nor
could be held accountable
for the crime. Yet to make her
bear the fruit he sowed in her
was not this birth
a violation?
Her body not her own,
a passageway for others
to enter, exit
not at her free will.

"It's my body," I said
when my father wanted
to extract a splinter,
painfully, from my finger.
"I'll do it."
I was fortunate, yet

you could stick pins
all over the country,
and each might reveal
some unvoiced, private tragedy:
a girl in a Leitrim churchyard,
two babies, in Kerry;

and others, mute
as cows in the field,
who birthed their load
with the tag
of 'sinfulness' tied on,

maidservants, agricultural girls
binding their stomachs,
hiding their babies
in hedges, under stones—
ghostly voices crying out,
keening themselves;

Like shamed ghosts on the old road
the girls behind the golf course
walk hidden from public places. Their guardians

seem dressed in mourning, tend
the terrible small graveyard
under dark trees. They know

that each birth forced and taken
scars the heart, deadens
a part of it, leaving
a trail of blood and mucus
leading
to the source, a defiled cavern.

Looking Between Buildings

Who made the walls,
built arches bricked up, walled up,
what calloused thumb
keyed in the square stone, what
fingers chose the one
best fitting the small gap?
Who laid stone that is
bone-white, heather coloured
marking boundaries, making
ramparts for the church
a bulwark against unbelievers?

Stone much more ancient
than the builders,
walls rearing like cliffs, crowding me,
unread pages of a lost script:
bleached stone;
stone like dried blood.

The Glen Park

Each end there was a vista of pylons
and the strata of grey houses, rising.
All the features were indicators of gloom:
the brown flesh of a mattress slumped at the streamside,
a trickle of rubbish down the ravine,
bare rock used as a scribbling board:
under gang markings, a faded crucifix.
The dead sky pressed down smoke
over the dull water the ducks quacked on.
Below scrubland, a thin man let his terrier
range over the birds' island,
disturbing them, rising them from nests.
No children played where you'd expect
adventurous games: safer in the half light
behind drawn curtains they are
motionless, only their eyes move
following flickering images on the video screen:
prison and salt tears their birthright.

Cape Clear in Spring

When we came back
it looked wetter, more woebegone,
there were clusters of
hartstongue fern that gleamed in the wet,
there was green slick on the wood,
the stones were precarious, looser.
In this Western climate
it does not take long
to unroof a building:
past sulphur gorse
lichen bearded cattle houses
and plants reclaimed men's work.
There was carmine-bulbed stonecrop,
and ruby, edging the green flesh
of navelwort. On cliff tops
rock whitened with ashy growth
had hollows like bone sockets.
Inland, wetland was a rushy arc
and light silvered the upper fields:
the sea molten beneath them, surging,
like a gaunt skull speaking, the rock.

Revisiting Ringabella

Would you say
a requiem for a rockpool
is scant subject for poetry?

What was crystal is
weed-choked, was defined
is slime traced
with bubbles of decay:

I think
nitrates had spilled
from farmland into the sea,

and any crystal-gazer
could see
that whatever is used to excess
moves to its opposite,
becomes cancerous,

but who could tell
new converts to science
who lately left
grove and holy well
that pishogues
made better sense?

In Himalaya
the Kamaris pray for health.
We, choosing wealth, may
die with the consequence:

and when land chokes
and the high snows
are smut-blackened, will we
come to our knees to
call to heaven with the Kamaris?

The aborigines
scarred men to make shamans.
Poets are scarred differently.
If we were healed, could we
speak freely?

Others have survived
frightful experience, touched
death and not died, travelled
distances and returned
to speak.